18599

599.74   Green, Carl R.
GRE

The striped skunk

$11.95

DATE			

THE STRIPED SKUNK

BY
CARL R. GREEN
WILLIAM R. SANFORD

EDITED BY
DR. HOWARD SCHROEDER, Ph.D.
**Professor in Reading and Language Arts
Dept. of Curriculum and Instruction
Mankato State University**

PRODUCED AND DESIGNED BY
BAKER STREET PRODUCTIONS
Mankato, MN

CRESTWOOD HOUSE
Mankato, Minnesota

LIBRARY OF CONGRESS CATALOGING IN PUBLICATION DATA
Green, Carl R.
The striped skunk.

(Wildlife, habits & habitat)
SUMMARY: Describes the physical characteristics, behavior, and natural environment of various types of skunks with emphasis on the most commonly seen striped skunk.
1. Striped skunk--Juvenile literature. (1. Striped skunk. 2. Skunks) I. Sanford, William R. (William Reynolds) II. Schroeder, Howard. III. Title. IV. Series.
QL737.C25S25   1987   599.74'447   87-6852
ISBN 0-89686-338-7

| International Standard Book Number: | Library of Congress Catalog Card Number: |
| Library Binding 0-89686-338-7 | 87-6852 |

ILLUSTRATION CREDITS:

Cover Photo: Lynn Rogers
Gary R. Zahm/DRK Photo: 5
Lynn Rogers: 6, 9, 14, 18, 22, 24-25, 32, 34, 38, 42
Gary Milburn/Tom Stack & Associates: 10
Leonard Lee Rue III: 13, 21, 28
T.J. Cawley/Tom Stack & Associates: 17
Thomas Kitchin/Tom Stack & Associates: 27, 37, 41, 45
Bob Williams: 46

CRESTWOOD HOUSE
Hwy. 66 South, Box 3427
Mankato, MN 56002-3427

TABLE OF CONTENTS

INTRODUCTION:

Grandmother Revere held the rowboat as Andrew stepped off the dock. When he was seated, she took her place at the oars. A moment later, the little boat was gliding across the calm waters of Long Island Sound. The first light of dawn showed in the east.

"Gram, why do we have to start so early?" Andrew asked.

"If we want fish for breakfast, we have to keep the same schedule they do," Gram replied. She pointed the boat toward the dim outlines of the Thimble Islands.

Andrew sniffed the breeze. "I smell a skunk," he said. "I think it's coming from one of the islands."

Gram wrinkled her nose. "That's a skunk, sure enough," she said. "Some dog probably thought it could eat a skunk for dinner. I bet it knows better now."

"If I ran into a skunk, I'd pick it up by the tail," Andrew told her. "Then it couldn't spray me."

"Ha!" Gram laughed. "Skunks can spray you from any position! Remember, a skunk's musk is its only real weapon. A skunk that thinks it's in danger will spray anything—even a bear. If a skunk stamps its feet, get out of the way. That's a warning. If you don't back away, it will curl into a U-shape with its back end pointing at you. That's the ready-to-fire position."

4

A striped skunk is in ready-to-fire position!

"With a weapon like that, skunks ought to be kings of the woods," Andrew said with a grin.

Gram shook her head. "A skunk won't go looking for a fight," she said. "But it won't back away from one, either."

The boat neared Palmer's Island. Andrew studied the rocky shore with his binoculars. To his delight, a striped skunk waddled down to the water. Carefully, the cat-sized animal dipped its paws into the water.

"Look!" Andrew whispered. "Can it spray us from there?"

"We'd have to be within twelve feet (3.7 m) to be in danger," Gram said. "But the smell can carry for twenty miles (32 km)!"

A skunk's range for spraying is about twelve feet (3.7 m).

Andrew studied the skunk's glossy black-and-white fur. "What happens when a skunk uses up its musk?" he wondered.

"A skunk can fire five to eight bursts before its musk glands run dry," Gram said. "Then the glands go to work again. Within a couple of hours, it will have musk for another shot or two."

"Is the musk poisonous?" Andrew asked.

"If a small animal swallowed liquid musk, it might die," Gram said. "More often, the liquid breaks into a spray that hits the target animal's eyes. The musk blinds the animal for an hour or two and gives the skunk plenty of time to escape."

Andrew watched the skunk as it stalked a mouse. "How do you know so much about skunks, Gram?" he asked.

"I used to trap them for their fur when I was your age," Gram said. "But one day a big male sprayed me from head to foot. I had to run home and scrub myself with ammonia to kill the smell. My dad burned my clothes and made me give up trapping after that."

"You must have looked funny, running from a skunk," Andrew chuckled. He laughed so hard the boat started rocking.

"Stop laughing and bait your hook, or we'll never catch our breakfast!" Gram scolded. "Tonight, if you're still eager to learn about skunks, we'll read about them in the Branford library."

CHAPTER ONE:

People never forget their first whiff of a skunk's musk. It doesn't matter whether the skunk was close or far away. The choking smell of a skunk's musk remains fresh in one's memory.

The skunk's names reflect this strong feeling. In German, the skunk is known as *stinktier*. The striped skunk's Latin name is *Mephitis*, which means "terrible smell." Similarly, spotted skunks are labeled as *putorius*, Latin for "a stinker." The names are accurate, but a little unfair. Skunks don't go looking for trouble. They only use their musk in self-defense.

The skunk also goes by a variety of common names. Some people call them wood-pussies, polecats, or civets. The last two names properly belong to the skunk's distant European relatives. True skunks live only in the Americas.

The mustelid family

Skunks belong to a family of mammals known as the *Mustelidae*. Other family members include otters, weasels, minks, and badgers. All of the mustelids produce musk from glands located at the base of their tails. But only skunks use their musk as a powerful weapon.

The skunk that most people see (and smell!) is the striped skunk *(Mephitis mephitis)*. Wherever you go in the United States and southern Canada, you can be sure that a striped skunk isn't far away. As with all skunks, the striped skunk wears a glossy black coat with white markings. Its head has a white "cap" and a stripe on the snout. Another stripe divides behind the head and runs along each side of the skunk's broad back. Finally, the striped skunk's bushy tail also is tipped with white.

The skunk's distinct markings make it easy to identify.

The spotted skunk is smaller than the striped skunk.

The spotted skunk *(Spilogale putorius)* is smaller, quicker, and more secretive. Its "spots" are really six wavy white stripes that are broken up into smaller patches. The white patches curve along the back, sides, and rump of the spotted skunk. The long black tail ends in a white tip. Spotted skunks climb trees to escape predators or to find food. If they can't avoid a fight, they often do a "handstand" on their front feet before "opening fire."

Hooded skunks *(Mephitis macroura)* live mostly in Mexico and Central America. They prefer dry, desert country. Hooded skunks look like striped skunks, except for narrower stripes and a "ruff" of white fur that covers their head and neck. Their tails are longer than their bodies. All skunks are good diggers, but hooded skunks are the best diggers of all.

South America's only skunk is the hog-nosed skunk *(Conepatus mesoleucus)*. Slow and sluggish, it ranges from the southwestern United States to the southern tip of South America. This skunk uses its strong front claws and flexible, bare snout to dig for insects. Its fur is coarse and stiff. Instead of stripes or spots, the hog-nosed skunk wears a mantle of white hair from the top of its head to the tip of its bushy tail. At first glance, the hog-nosed skunk looks as though it's covered with snow.

Cat-sized and long-tailed

Skunks are short-legged, long-tailed animals. A typical male striped skunk measures twenty-five to thirty-two inches (64 to 81 cm) in length. Of that, ten to twelve inches (25 to 30 cm) is tail. The same male stands about eight inches (20 cm) tall at the shoulder and weighs five to ten pounds (2.3 to 4.5 kg).

The smaller spotted skunks average twelve to twenty-two inches (30 to 56 cm) in length. They also have shorter tails. A typical spotted skunk weighs two to three pounds (0.9 to 1.4 kg). In both varieties, the females are ten to twenty percent smaller than the males. The weight of both sexes varies with the season.

A black-and-white signal

Naturalists believe the skunk's black-and-white coat is a warning signal to other animals. The white markings show clearly at night, when the skunk does its hunting. Most predators stay out of the skunk's path once they see or smell it.

A skunk's fur grows in two layers. The outer coat of guard hair is one to three inches (2.5 to 7.5 cm) long. The white guard hair is longer than the black. The thick, kinky hair of the undercoat is three-quarters to one and one-half inches (2 to 4 cm) long. The undercoat adds extra protection from rain and cold. Each spring, the skunk loses its winter coat and grows a new one.

A skunk's tail has guard hairs that grow as long as six or seven inches (15 to 18 cm). When the skunk is frightened or angry, its tail bristles and expands to twice its usual size. This is another of the skunk's warning signals.

When frightened or angry, a skunk's tail expands to twice its normal size.

The musk glands are found below the base of the tail.

A smelly defense

Skunks make their musk in two glands that lie below the base of the tail. When an enemy comes too close, a nipple pops out on each side of the anus. Strong muscles then squirt the oily yellow musk from the nipples. The skunk can spray it as a stream or as a fine mist.

The musk's chemical name is *butylmercaptan.* A

14

Canadian naturalist describes it as "a mixture of strong ammonia, essence of garlic, burning sulphur, a volume of sewer gas, a sulphuric acid spray, [and] a dash of perfume musk." Very few animals can endure close contact with this smelly fluid.

By the time they're a month old, skunk kittens can squirt tiny streams of musk. As adults, they can fire up to eight bursts before running out of musk. Even then, a skunk always seems to have a tiny bit left for one last squirt. The glands go to work to make a new supply almost at once.

Short legs and sharp teeth

A skunk will never win a gold medal for speed. Its short legs and five-toed paws are better equipped for digging and food gathering. Each paw is tipped with sharp claws. Unlike a cat, the skunk cannot pull in its claws. The one-inch (2.5 cm) front claws are longer than the back claws and are curved for digging.

Striped skunks use three gaits: a walk, a canter, and an awkward gallop. The walk is slow, for a skunk usually stops every few steps to dig for grubs and worms. If it's in a hurry, the skunk canters at about four miles (6.4 km) an hour. In a real emergency, the skunk shifts into an eight mph (12.8 kmph) gallop. A galloping skunk tires quickly, and froths at the mouth. In most cases, however, the skunk doesn't have to run. One whiff of musk sends most predators hurrying away.

A skunk's long jaws hold thirty-four teeth. These include twelve incisors (cutting teeth), four canines (piercing or holding teeth), and eighteen premolars and molars (grinding teeth). Skunks use their razor-sharp incisors to kill small mammals and reptiles with a single bite on the head or neck. Like dogs, they use their premolars to chew off chunks of meat.

Finding food by odor

Skunks have keen noses and sharp ears. They depend mostly on their sense of smell to find food and to avoid danger. A thick pad protects their noses when they're rooting around in the dirt. Skunks also rely on their ears, which are hidden under their long neck hair. A female skunk, for example, finds a lost kitten by listening for its cries.

The skunk sees well at close range, but its eyesight is poor beyond twenty feet (6 m). If an object isn't moving, the skunk doesn't seem to see it. On the positive side, the skunk's black, shiny eyes adjust to both darkness and daylight. Like many nocturnal animals, however, a skunk is color-blind. Eyes that see well at

Skunks are color-blind, but they can see very well at night.

night lack the cone-shaped cells needed to see color.

Despite their lack of size and speed, skunks aren't on the endangered species list. In fact, more skunks live in North America today than lived here in the 1600's. As the wilderness disappears, these small animals adjust to a variety of habitats.

CHAPTER TWO:

One variety of skunks or another can be found from Hudson Bay in Canada to Tierra del Fuego in South America. All of the states in the United States have skunks, except for Alaska and Hawaii. Across that vast range, skunks inhabit woodlands, deserts, farmlands, and built-up urban areas. Because these small mustelids prefer lowlands, they seldom live above six thousand feet (1,830 m).

Unlike most wild animals, skunks don't move out when people move in. In fact, they seem to prefer open fields to forests and heavily wooded areas. Female skunks also raise their litters beneath peoples' houses. The owners may not know the skunks are there until a foolish dog forces the skunks to use their musk.

Skunks prefer to live in open areas.

Live and let live

Striped skunks prefer a solitary life. Each animal goes its own way, crossing paths with other skunks but seldom socializing. When two males fight, they're competing for a female, not for territory. Where food is plentiful, naturalists find as many as 140 skunks per square mile (2.59 sq. km).

Although they're solitary animals, skunks are anything but quiet. When they're searching for food, they make a snuffling sound. Every once in a while, they clear their nose by sneezing. Skunks also squeak, growl, screech, coo, and hiss. Young skunks tend to be noisier than adult skunks.

A favorite habitat

If skunks could talk, they'd ask for a wooded hillside habitat near a pasture. A hillside provides good drainage for their dens during wet weather. At the same time, the pasture produces a rich crop of grubs, grasshoppers, and other insects. Hungry skunks crisscross the land each night, searching for food. They may travel two miles or more between sunset and sunrise.

Striped skunks spend the daylight hours in their dens. A skunk can dig its own den, but seems just as happy to use a den dug by a woodchuck or a fox. Skunks also use hollow tree stumps and small caves for dens. Females prefer dens that are protected from predators by tree roots or rocks. In settled areas, skunks also set up dens under houses and barns. Once a skunk uses a den, most other animals stay away from it.

Striped skunks do not always use the same den, but spotted skunks return to a favorite burrow. Young striped skunks often sleep outside during the summer months. They curl up under piles of brush, in heavy grass, or beneath an old tractor. Females will share a den, but males seldom do.

A varied diet

A skunk will eat almost anything, but it prefers insects. One study showed that a skunk eats large numbers of grasshoppers, crickets, grubs, cutworms, weevils, spiders, caterpillars, and other insects. To go with its diet of insects, it adds fruit, vegetables, and bird and turtle eggs. A skunk also eats mice and other rodents if it can catch them.

All skunks are clever food gatherers. If they develop a taste for honey, they will tear a hive apart to reach the honeycomb. Bee stings don't seem to bother them. Skunks also eat fuzzy caterpillars—but first they roll the insects on the ground to break off the poisonous bristles. Once in a while, a spotted skunk invades a chicken house to eat eggs and kill chickens. In urban

This striped skunk has found a nest of snapping turtle eggs to eat.

areas, homeowners may find cone-shaped holes in their lawns. That's a sign that a striped skunk has been digging for its favorite grubs and worms.

Despite the problems skunks create, many farmers like to have them around. The insects, mice, and other pests that skunks eat more than make up for the damage they do. Skunks also perform a cleanup service in nature. They eat the rotting flesh of dead animals.

A well-adapted animal

Skunks are well-adapted to their varied habitats. They seldom become excited or nervous. When they meet a predator, they stand their ground and warn the other animal to stay away. If the predator retreats, they go about their business. If the predator attacks, skunks usually win the fight with a salvo of musk.

Skunks don't like water, but they will swim a short distance. If it's raining, they shake themselves like dogs do, and get on with the nightly hunt for food. When skunks venture out on a warm day, their dark coats sometimes cause them to overheat. If that happens, they seek out a patch of shade and rest for a while.

A skunk can't stay in the sun very long. With its sun-absorbing black fur, it will overheat.

For animals that are alone much of the time, skunks live active social lives. If a kitten loses its mother, another female will adopt it. Young skunks love to play, and even older skunks may join in. Sometimes they do handstands just for the fun of it. As noted earlier, adult skunks share their territory and food sources. During the winter, several females may join a single male in a cozy den. In addition, skunks don't give up easily. They will work and work to reach fruit that is hanging just out of reach.

Like older people, adult skunks seem to value peace and quiet. They will often leave a noisy habitat, or one where the danger from predators has become too great.

Few natural enemies

Despite their strong defense, skunks do have natural enemies. Badgers sometimes dig into winter dens, for example. A powerful badger can kill a half dozen sleepy skunks in just a few minutes. Similarly, great horned owls sweep down and carry skunks back to their nests. Birds have a poor sense of smell, so the musk doesn't bother the owl very much. In addition, owls have special eyelids that protect their eyes from the stinging liquid. If they're hungry enough, eagles, coyotes, foxes, bobcats, cougars, and fishers also kill skunks for food.

Skunks have few natural enemies.

24

In urban areas, domestic dogs and cats prey on skunks. It takes a direct hit in the eyes to convince a dog that it should let a skunk go. Even after it's been sprayed, a dog will return later to try again. The small size of most house cats restricts them to attacks on younger skunks.

Even though skunks are clean animals, they're bothered by fleas, lice, flies, ticks, and mosquitoes. Insect pests and parasites cause several diseases. Rabies is the most serious disease that affects skunks, because it also kills people. Naturalists warn that all wild skunks are possible carriers of this fatal disease. Skunks also die from distemper, tularemia, and several other diseases. A wild skunk that survives all of these dangers can expect to live about six years.

Most skunks are killed by people

People kill skunks for a number of reasons. Until recently, hunters trapped the animals for their fur. Luckily for skunks, their fur has lost much of its popularity. Today, many skunks die under the wheels of speeding cars. Caught out on the road, skunks can't move fast enough to escape a car or truck. In addition, skunks sometimes eat the poison set out for coyotes, ground squirrels, or rats.

Other skunks are killed on purpose. If some chickens have been killed, or if there has been an outbreak of rabies, skunks may get the blame. When that happens, people use traps and poison to kill as many skunks as possible. A few people even kill skunks because they don't like their smell. These people forget that skunks play an important role in the cycle of life.

Sometimes people forget the importance of the skunk in the balance of nature.

CHAPTER THREE:

When winter comes, humans adjust easily to the cold. Adults turn up the furnace and children put on snowsuits.

Wild animals can't control their environment the way people do. When winter comes, they must find a way to survive the long, cold months. Skunks are no exception.

When winter comes, skunks move into a den.

Winter: A time to stay in the den

Skunks that live in warm climates remain active all year long. In the snowy woods of New England, however, a female striped skunk is sleeping in her den. With the temperature well below freezing, she could not survive in the open. On this December night, she is curled up with three other females and a big male. Not far away, a male skunk is sharing a den with an opossum. Neither animal seems troubled by its unusual bedfellow.

The skunk's body temperature holds steady at 99.5 degrees F. (37.4 degrees C.). This tells naturalists that the skunk is sleeping, not hibernating. Bears and other hibernating animals show a marked drop in body temperature.

The females almost never leave the den. When the weather warms up for a few days in January, the male waddles out to find food. This time he's lucky. A dead quail, shot by a hunter, has been left lying nearby. The male digs the bird out of the snow and eats his fill. The females hardly stir when he returns to the den.

By spring, the skunks will have lost thirty percent of what they weighed in the fall. One young female didn't fatten up enough. Like many one-year-olds, she will die of starvation before the spring thaw.

In late February, the old male becomes restless. He

senses that the mating season is coming. A few days later, a younger male crawls into the den, looking for a mate. The old male rams his shoulder into the younger skunk and bites at his legs. As if by agreement, neither uses his musk. After a brief battle, the younger male retreats, dragging one bloody leg. All through the woods, other males are out looking for females.

Mating takes place in early March. The male bites the female on the neck and holds her down beside him. At first she fights back, but she soon gives in. They mate several times over the next few days. A week later, the female drives the male away. Instinct tells her not to trust any male around the young to which she will soon give birth.

Spring: A time for raising a family

The female skunk carries her kittens within her for nine weeks before giving birth. She prepares the den by dragging in piles of grass and leaves. In early May, she gives birth to six kittens. This is a typical litter, but some females have as many as sixteen kittens. Each newborn weighs about one ounce (28 grams) and is three to four inches (7.6 to 10 cm) long. The kittens are born with their eyes and ears closed. Although they're tooth-less and hairless, the black-and-white pattern shows on their skin.

The kittens begin nursing thirty minutes after they're born. This female has twelve teats, but other females have anywhere from eleven to fourteen teats. In a litter of six, all of the kittens have a chance to nurse. In larger litters, the stronger kittens crowd out the weaker ones.

The kittens develop rapidly. When they're a month old, they weigh six to seven ounces (170 to 198 grams). Their eyes and ears are open, and they tumble playfully around the den. Two weeks later, their first teeth break through.

Summer: An exciting time for kittens

On a June night, the kittens leave the den with their mother. They follow her in single file. She catches grasshoppers and shares them with the kittens. They already know about insects, because the female has been bringing food back to the den for a week or more. She is molting, and has begun to wean them from her milk. The kittens soon begin catching their own food.

The young skunks also learn that the woods are full of danger. One night, a horned owl swoops down and

Young skunks, called kittens, learn to take care of themselves as they grow up.

grabs a kitten in her talons. The female turns and fires her musk, but it's too late. The owl flaps away, holding the dead kitten. On the way to the den that same night, the skunks run into a large dog. The kittens quickly curl into a defensive stance. The female has more range. She gives the dog a long, accurate squirt of musk. Blinded, the dog yelps and stumbles off toward home. Calmly, the female leads the kittens back to the den.

Day by day, the kittens learn their lessons. They dig

for grubs, find turtle eggs, and groom their coats to keep clean. At three months, the little family begins to split up. The young females sleep with their mother, but go off by themselves to find food. The males wander off to find dens of their own.

One male kitten falls into a trapper's steel trap. The trapper finds him and tries to set him free. The frightened skunk doesn't know he's being rescued. Just as his leg comes loose from the trap, the skunk sprays the man with musk. Then he limps off to hide in his den.

Fall: A time to prepare for winter's cold

The early fall fields are full of good things to eat. Instinctively, the skunks know they must gain weight for the winter that lies ahead. Along with insects, the skunks add berries, nuts, and cereal grains to their diet. They check out the roadsides, looking for animals killed by automobiles. A female strays onto the road and dies under the skidding wheels of a pickup truck.

The weather begins to turn cold. The skunks waddle out each night, protected by new layers of fat. One of them eats cabbages in a farmer's garden. Another finds an apple tree and fills up on fallen fruit. The two female kittens return to the den with their mother. They'll have

When the weather starts to get cold in the late fall, skunks spend more time looking for food.

a better chance of living through the winter if they share her body heat. Not far away, two young males share a den with a family of raccoons.

At last, the cold and snow drive the skunks underground. The old male is the last to enter his den. A farmer trudges by on snowshoes and smiles when he sees the tracks. He knows that the ''wood-pussies'' eat insects and rodents that could ruin his crops. Sharing the land with skunks and other wild animals seems like a natural thing to do.

CHAPTER FOUR:

Americans have lived side-by-side with skunks for thousands of years. The word "skunk" probably comes from the animal's Algonquin Indian name, *segonku*. Even place names can be traced back to this small, smelly mustelid. Chicago, for example, takes its name from the Fox Indian word for "place of the skunk."

An animal of myth and practical uses

The American Indians told many stories about the skunk. Indian parents, for example, warned children not to complain or make faces when they smelled a skunk. The children were taught that their hair would turn white if they ignored this lesson! Another myth claimed that someone would die if skunk kittens were born in a den under an Indian's home.

Both the Indians and European settlers found practical uses for the skunk. The Indians made warm clothing from the fur and stew from the meat. The settlers who tried skunk meat reported that it was sweet and tender. The settlers also learned to make a medicine from skunk fat. They used the oil to treat whooping cough, asthma, and other breathing problems. In addition, a bit of skunk musk was once used as a base for perfumes! That comes as a surprise to anyone who has smelled the musk at full strength.

Would you wear a skunk jacket?

In modern times, stylish women wore coats made of skunk fur. Of course, the furriers never called it by its real name. They sold skunk fur as ''Alaskan sable'' or ''black marten.'' When new laws required proper labeling, however, the public stopped buying. No one seemed to want a ''skunk'' jacket. The price of a skunk fur fell to less than a dollar (US).

When ''fun furs'' became stylish in the 1980's, the price rose again. Striped skunk pelts now sell for about $5 (US) and spotted skunk pelts for $15 (US). The furriers first treat the fur with chemicals to remove the ''skunky'' smell. Then they dye the white stripes to make an all-black fur. Even though skunk furs are quite luxurious, most fur buyers prefer mink or ermine.

Treating the smell of musk

What can you do if you're sprayed by a skunk? As John Audubon, the great American naturalist, once said: ''Even the bravest of our boasting race is, by this little

A person might as well throw their clothes away after being sprayed by a skunk!

animal, compelled to break off his train of thoughts, hold his nose, and run—as if a lion were at his heels.'' One old bit of wisdom suggests that you ''wash your clothes, bury them for a week, and then wash them again. After that, throw them away!''

Experts agree that there's no perfect solution. They suggest a good scrubbing with ammonia (add a cup of ammonia to each gallon of water). Other people say that tomato juice is a good ''de-skunker.'' Dog owners pour cans of tomato juice over their pets and then wash them with mint-scented shampoo. After that, they keep the dog outside until the odor finally fades away!

Skunks do not make good pets, because they never become completely tame.

The skunk as a pet

People who want an unusual pet can buy a skunk from a pet store. Since skunks can't be trained not to use their musk, veterinarians have to remove the musk glands. When well handled, pet skunks are playful and cuddly. They keep themselves clean, and they learn to use a litter box. Skunk owners enjoy the surprised looks they receive when they take their pets for a walk.

Some doctors warn that pet skunks should be vaccinated against rabies. This fatal disease is common in wild skunks. However, if the skunk is already infected with rabies, the vaccine can prolong the skunk's life for several years. The vaccine doesn't get rid of the disease. If the skunk bites its owner, the owner could get rabies. The vaccine is safe to use only if the owner knows that the skunk is not infected with rabies.

Even when they're de-scented and vaccinated, skunks don't make perfect pets. For one thing, they never become fully tame. They may not be able to spray you, but their teeth are razor sharp. As with their wild cousins, pet skunks tend to be more active at night. They're most awake when you're ready for bed. Because they'll eat almost anything, overfeeding can also be a problem.

People who keep a pet skunk have a last lesson to learn: A de-scented skunk can never return to the wild. Left without its musk, a skunk would be easy prey for any predator.

CHAPTER FIVE:

Life in the Colorado mountains was exciting for the young couple. Tom was writing a new book assignment, and Carol was preparing for their first baby. The fall air was fresh, the sky was a deep blue, and only the wind in the trees broke the quiet. Best of all, Carol thought, were the animals.

Each day, she put a plate of scraps outside the cabin. At first, only the blue jays visited the plate. Then a pair of squirrels raced in and grabbed the stale bread. Carol watched them with a sense of wonder. Who would come next?

A black-and-white visitor

She didn't have long to wait. Two nights later, a small black-and-white animal waddled up to the cabin. Carol was sitting by the window. "Tom! We've got a visitor," she whispered. "Unless I'm dreaming, there's a striped skunk out there."

The skunk sniffed at the plate and picked up a crust of bread. It ate slowly and daintily. Then it walked away. Carol let out her breath. The only thing she knew about skunks was that they sprayed musk all over anyone who upset them.

To Carol's delight, the skunk returned the next evening. "He seems safe enough," she told Tom. "Besides, how do you tell a skunk to go away? I'm going to call him Luke." If the squirrels beat him to the plate, Luke waited for Carol to fill it again. She found that he liked dog chow better than stale bread.

A winter den

When cold weather hit, Luke found a warm den under the cabin. Tom didn't like the idea of a skunk living

Skunks will look for a warm place to live when the weather turns cold.

beneath them, but he didn't know how to evict him.

A few nights later, Carol heard strange noises under the floor. "There's more than one animal down there," she told Tom.

The next day, Tom crawled under the cabin to see what was living there. His flashlight showed that Luke had company! A family of raccoons and another skunk had joined him. Tom decided it was safest to ignore the sleeping animals.

Carol often saw paw prints in the snow. Luke and his friend sometimes went down to the stream for water when the weather was good. They also ate the food she

These tracks in the snow were made by a skunk.

put out for them. Finally, the snow piled up on the roads and Tom became worried about Carol. He took her back to the city to be closer to the doctor.

Their baby was born in April, just as the snow was melting in the mountains. A month later, Tom took Carol and the baby back to the cabin. After living in the mountains, they both felt that the city was too busy and noisy.

"Luke" gives birth

Luke was nowhere to be seen. Then Carol heard something squeaking under the floor. She told Tom that rats were nesting down there. Tom said "Don't worry," and crawled under the cabin with his flashlight. He came back with a big smile on his face.

"You'll have to change Luke's name to Lucy," he told her. "Your little friend has given birth to a litter of kittens!"

Carol put out food, and Lucy dragged it back to her den. Three weeks later, she led her seven kittens on their first trip to the food dish. The tiny kittens ate like a gang of black-and-white piglets. Carol had to put out a second dish for Lucy.

From her window, Carol saw Lucy take her young ones on "field trips" to the stream and the woods. The kittens walked in single file behind her, like tiny circus elephants. They dug for grubs and caught crickets.

Sometimes they did handstands on their front paws and rolled around like playful puppies.

On another day, Lucy led the kittens to a nearby hillside. Carol followed and saw them looking into some empty burrows. "The family is shopping for new dens," she told Tom that night.

Nature can be cruel

Tom came back from a shopping trip a week later to find Carol crying. "What's wrong?" he asked. "Is the baby sick?"

"Mikey is fine," she said. "It's Lucy and her kittens. They have a terrible disease. Two of them are dead and the others won't eat. Can't we do something to help?"

Tom went out to take a look. He was shaking his head when he came back. "I think they have distemper," he said sadly. "There's nothing we can do. It's part of nature's balancing act. If every kitten grew up and mated, we'd be overrun with skunks."

Carol nodded. "I'll say a prayer for the kittens that are still alive," she said.

One of the kittens did survive. Carol named him Lucky. As time passed, Lucky began to wander off by himself each night. For a while he returned to the den each morning. Finally, he didn't come back at all.

Lucy didn't seem to mind. She went about her daily

routine of feeding, grooming, and sleeping. One night a fox followed her under the house. Lucy drove the fox away with several bursts of musk. The odor drifted up into the cabin. Carol and Tom decided to sleep in the car that night.

Carol hugged Mikey and thought about Lucy and her kittens. The heavy scent of musk seemed to have followed her to the car. "Lucy's just doing what comes naturally," she sighed. "It's a truly awful smell, I know. But life in the mountains wouldn't be the same without these beautiful, stinky creatures."

The skunk is a beautiful creature, even if it is "stinky" at times!

MAP:

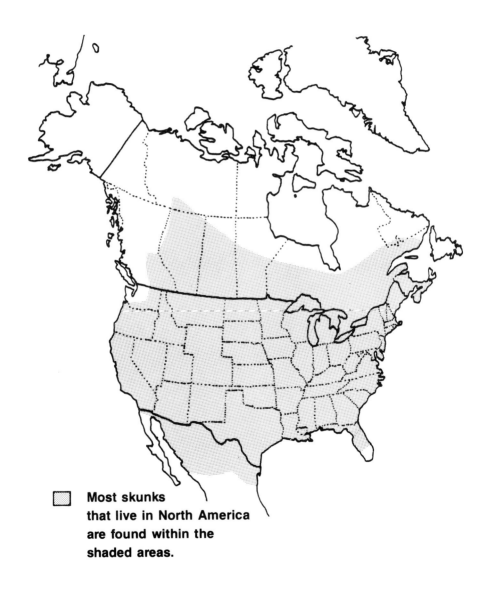

Most skunks that live in North America are found within the shaded areas.

INDEX/GLOSSARY:

WILDLIFE
HABITS & HABITAT

If you would like to know more about all kinds of wildlife, you should take a look at the other books in this series.

You'll find books on bald eagles and other birds. Books on alligators and other reptiles. There are books about deer and other big-game animals. And there are books about sharks and other creatures that live in the ocean.

In all of the books you will learn that life in the wild is not easy. But you will also learn what people can do to help wildlife survive. So read on!